The Tragedy of Moses

by

Elliott Kanbar

ELBAR Associates, LLC
PO Box 20038
New York, NY 10075

ISBN 0-692-84464-3
EAN 978-0-692-84464-9
Library of Congress Control Number: 2016918317
Printed in the United States of America

Table of Contents

Introduction

The story of Moses first intrigued me when I was a student at the Yeshiva Etz Chaim in Borough Park, Brooklyn. For eight years, we studied Torah in the morning and took English courses in the afternoon. It was during those years that I started to question the many inconsistencies I felt appeared in the Biblical narrative. Why did God wait 400 years before rescuing the Israelites? Why did He try to murder Moses on his way to Egypt? Why did Aaron get a free pass, even though he was the ringleader in the Golden Calf fiasco? Why wasn't he punished for his failed attempt to overthrow Moses? And, the question that pops up all the time, why didn't God allow Moses, his trusted and loyal friend, to enter The Promised Land?

The Orthodox rabbis at the Yeshiva were troubled by my questions. Their response was always the same: "God has his reasons."

As an adult, I gravitated to the Reform side of Judaism. The rabbis were more tolerant and often amused by my questions, never angry. But their answers were also always the same: "The Torah was not written by God. It was written by people. Don't take it literally."

In the entire recording of Biblical history, the story that most riveted me was the tragedy of Moses. He gave it his all, talked "face to face" with an irascible God, was loyal to the nth degree, survived forty years in the harsh Sinai desert, struggled with a bunch of unruly Israelites, and always, always did God's bidding. He finally reached the door to The Promised Land. But there he was coldly and brutally refused entry by a God who held a grudge for a trivial act of disobedience. This is a tragedy if ever there was one.

Finally, exhausted from the many disputes with devout friends about these Biblical issues, I sat down to write this book.

I tried to view these Biblical events through a contemporary lens. When Moses massacred the Midianites, I wondered whether his Midianite wife, Zipporah, would have divorced him and demanded alimony. Preposterous? Maybe. But that is certainly what might happen today.

I also wanted to avoid, under penalty of death, writing a discourse that was ponderous and pedantic. I thus opted to tell the story of Moses in verse. It also seemed like the right way to go because the Torah is often recited in a sing-song manner.

I must confess that hosting the syndicated radio show, "Wild About Broadway" for four years motivated me to try my hand writing verse. How can one not be inspired studying the great lyricists like Stephen Sondheim, Oscar Hammerstein II,

E.Y. Harburg, Johnny Mercer, Sheldon Harnick, Cole Porter, and more recently, Lin-Manuel Miranda ("Hamilton").

I hope this book arouses some questions in your mind. I also hope it results in a few friendly discussions with friends and relatives. After all, that is my intention.

Elliott Kanbar
New York City
2016

Cast of Characters

LEADER, the narrator of our tale

ISRAELITES, five representatives of the emancipated slaves

PHARAOH, Egypt's ruthless leader, who enslaved the Israelites

ADVISORS TO PHARAOH, the men who do PHARAOH's bidding

JOSEPH, son of Jacob, sold by his brothers into slavery

JACOB, Joseph's father, who brings the Israelites to Egypt

GOD, our irascible creator

BITYA, daughter of PHARAOH

JOCHEBED and AMRAM, mother and father of MOSES, AARON, and MIRIAM

JOSHUA, lieutenant to MOSES

JETHRO, father of ZIPPORAH and father-in-law to MOSES

AARON, brother of MOSES

SCOUTS, agents who report to MOSES

CALEB, a scout

MIRIAM, sister of MOSES

KORAH, leader of a rebellion against MOSES

ISRAELITE SOLDIERS, members of MOSES'S army

1

In the Beginning

LEADER:

It's fitting,
while we're sitting,
to tell the story
of the tragedy of Moses
right from the beginning.

ISRAELITE #1:

Of liberation!

ISRAELITE #2:

Of emancipation!

ISRAELITE #3:

And creation!

ISRAELITE #4:

Of an Israelite nation!

LEADER:

Joseph, favorite son of Jacob,
sold by his jealous brothers
to an Ishmaelite caravan,
for 20 pieces of silver.
Ended up in Egypt.
But Joseph could sure deliver,
good with dreams,
so it seems;
knew what they meant,
saw their portent,
became Pharaoh's hero,
in the know,
part of the palace clan.
That's how it began.

PHARAOH:

I love Joseph,
so cool, no fool.
He saved us from starvation—
elation!
Joseph will be Lord of our nation.

JOSEPH to JACOB:

Father and brothers,
starving in Canaan,
I forgive,
live and let live.
Pack up your stuff,
gather your flock.

Take stock.
Don't miss a beat,
come to Egypt.
Here, with me, you'll eat.

PHARAOH to JOSEPH:

Joseph, it's crystal clear,
bring your family here.
It's grand;
we'll settle them in Goshen,
the fat of the land.

Source and Commentary: The malevolent sale of
Joseph by his brothers to the passing Ishmaelite
caravan heading for Egypt is described in Genesis
37: 18-36. Joseph's roller coaster adventures in
Egypt are covered vividly and with thoroughness in
Genesis 39-44. When famine struck Canaan,
Joseph's brothers came to Egypt seeking help.
Joseph recognized them and forgave them, an
incredible act of mercy. This gives full meaning to
the old saying that "The key to happiness is a bad
memory."

2

Jacob's Lament

JACOB to GOD:

Dear God,
I'm perplexed,
vexed.

My son Joseph wants us all
to trek to Egypt
and live with him
in a strange land.

I'm not sure.
Shall I go?
Or take it slow?
You told Abraham
we'll be slaves for 400 years
in a strange land.
I have many fears.

Canaan is our home.
Is it wise now to roam?
To travel to a distant land,
to the unknown?

You commanded Isaac,
"Stay in Canaan.
You will be fertile;
you will prosper."

Tell me what to do?
Give me a sign.
What shall I do?
So now I'm packed,
ready to move on.
Will I get sacked?
Should I cross the line?
Dear God, give me a sign!

GOD to JACOB:

Jacob,
go to your son in Egypt.
Gather your crew,
I will be with you.
I'll hold your hand;
next to you I'll stand.
Go to Egypt, stay on track,
and this I promise:
I'll bring you back.

LEADER:

And they all came to Egypt,
settled in the land of Goshen,
happy to be there.
Without a worry or a care,
they were fertile and healthy,
became wealthy.
Will this change?
Was coming to Egypt a mistake?
Or a heartbreak?

Source and Commentary: A shocker in this narrative is that God, a long time before, had told Abraham that his descendants would be slaves in a strange land for 400 years (Genesis 15:13). The basis for this prognostication has baffled Biblical scholars. If God did foresee this, why did he encourage Jacob to go to Egypt? God did promise Jacob to bring him back (Genesis 46: 1-4). After 400 years? Jacob's hesitations, God's assurances, and the final journey to Egypt are described in Genesis 45: 16-25 and 46: 1-4. Interestingly, God did not give Isaac the same advice he gave Jacob; instead he encouraged Isaac to remain in Canaan (Genesis 26: 2-4).

3

Egypt Before Moses

LEADER:

Joseph died;
an evil Pharaoh sits on the throne.
The Israelites are alone.
No protection.
Much apprehension.

To this Pharaoh,
Joseph is nothing.
Joseph is history.
And the Israelites will experience misery.

PHARAOH to ADVISORS:

Advisors, we need to meet.
I've heard on the street
that the Israelites are multiplying.
It's a worry,
Hurry!

ADVISORS to PHARAOH:

What can we do?
Whom do we sue?

PHARAOH:

Enslave them all—
do it now!
Don't stall.

ADVISORS:

Free labor.
We like that.
We'll get them in line—
you can put that in your hat.

LEADER:

Years later.

PHARAOH to ADVISORS:

These Israelite slaves
continue to multiply.
Now they've got to die.
The girls can live.
The boys must die.
Do as I say—
obey!

LEADER:

Jochabed and Amram, an Israelite couple,
gave birth to a son.
If the Egyptians find him,
he's gone.
Put him in a basket.
Float him down the Nile.
No time to prance;
gotta take a chance.
Going for a swim,
Bitya, Pharaoh's daughter,
finds him.
Lucky day.
He'll be okay.

BITYA to MAIDENS:

What joy!
Finding this gorgeous boy.
But he's an Israelite.
Will I be able to keep him?
Chances slim.
Have to convince Daddy.
It's sink or swim.

Source and Commentary: Exodus 1: 8-22 & Exodus
2: 1-10. In the Torah, Pharaoh's daughter has no
name. A few Biblical scholars eventually gave her
the name Bitya. It's an outrage that she never
received full credit for her enormous courage. Bitya
bucked her father's hard-and-fast rule to kill all

male Israelite babies. She saved Moses from sure death. Without Bitya, there would be no Moses.

4

Pharaoh and Bitya

LEADER:

The dreaded moment arrived when Bitya confronted
her father about the Israelite baby boy she had
fetched from the Nile.

BITYA:

It won't be easy.
I'm feeling queasy.

PHARAOH:

Bitya, dear,
was that a baby crying last night?
Was I dreaming?
Or am I right?

BITYA:

Listen to this:
I was bathing in the Nile.
A wicker basket with a baby floated by,
looked like it had dropped from the sky.

PHARAOH:

What are you smoking?
Are you high?
He's an Israelite baby—
he's got to die.

BITYA:

Hold on, Daddy.
He's so cute, so nice.
Let's keep him,
let's take a chance—
let's roll the dice.

PHARAOH:

He's a baby now,
I vow,
he'll grow up somehow.
An enemy he'll be,
You'll see.
Don't ask why,
this baby must die.

BITYA:

I have given him a name:
Moses.
If he's gonna die,
so will I.

PHARAOH:

One day, he'll destroy us.
We're gonna fall.
But you're my daughter,
so, okay,
it's your call.

Commentary: The Torah makes no mention of any discussion between Bitya and her father after she brings baby Moses to the palace. I've always wished I were a fly on the wall and able to listen to what went on. I can only surmise that she was amazingly persuasive to convince her ruthless father into keeping Moses, though it's all conjecture on my part. But what remains as fact is that Pharaoh's daughter was a true savior and should have been revered by Biblical historians. Unfortunately, that is not the case, to this day.

5

Mother and Moses

LEADER:

The Torah mentions nothing about the adventures of Moses growing up in the palace. But there's reason to believe he made periodic contact with his mother, Jochebed. Later he would reunite with his brother Aaron and sister Miriam. This explains his feeling that, despite his Egyptian upbringing, he was, at heart, an Israelite. Here we can imagine one of their exchanges:

MOSES to JOCHEBED:

No more talk.
I'm goin' for a walk.

JOCHEBED:

Moses,
you are not a star.
Remember who you are.

MOSES:

Don't spoil it for me.
This is where I belong.
I feel free.

When I walk by the Nile,
my subjects bow.
Wow!

JOCHEBED:

You've come far,
but remember who you are.

MOSES:

To Pharaoh,
I'm his son.
We talk, we eat,
we have fun.

JOCHEBED:

Be careful, Moses.
While you're living well,
your people
are living in hell.

Pharaoh's not the man you think—
he'll kill us one day.
All we can do is pray.

Commentary: It's quite possible that a conversation like this could have happened. Mothers are supposed to tell their children what to do. Most of the times, children don't listen. It took a killing to force Moses to see the light.

6

Moses Slays the Egyptian

LEADER: Moses, it seems, was enjoying the good life in Pharaoh's palace. But one day his life changed. Big time.

MOSES:

Talk about a life-changing event—
taking a morning stroll,
then torment.

I see this Egyptian taskmaster
beating a Hebrew slave,
and I see red.
Look left, look right—
nobody's in sight.
This Egyptian dude
is goin' to be dead.

LEADER:

Moses struck the Egyptian with what, we don't know, but it was hard enough to kill him.

MOSES:

If Pharaoh hears about it,
I'm dead meat.
Better get on my feet
and split.

I was Lord of the Land,
but now I'm heading for the hinterland.

So long, Egypt;
hello, Midian.

Source and Commentary: Exodus 2: 11-15. To this day there is much debate among Biblical scholars about whether Moses commits murder in this passage. The fact that he "looked right and looked left" before striking the Egyptian would be damaging to Moses's defense in a court of law. This event does reveal that modest, gentle Moses also has a brutal side. This aspect of Moses's character will flare up again as he deals harshly with his unruly people in the Sinai wilderness and ruthlessly destroys his enemies during the journey.

7

Moses in Midian

LEADER:

Moses fled from Pharaoh and dwelt in the land of
Midian. Midian was somewhere in the southwest
corner of present-day Jordan, alongside the Gulf of
Aqaba.

MOSES:

The Midianites were my cure,
kind and loving.
I felt secure.
Jethro gave me a job.
I cared for his flock.
Never watched the clock.
He had seven daughters,
Zipporah the fairest of them all.
Man, we had a ball.
Married her,
I was happy,
I was free,
but I knew I had to move on.
Then God paid me a visit.
Am I gone?
Is this it?

Source and Commentary: Exodus 2: 15-22. It's hard to pin down exactly who were these Midianites who saved Moses from execution by Pharaoh. Some say they were distant relatives of the Israelites, and that might explain their kindness to Moses. But Jethro, Moses's father-in-law and benefactor, was deemed a pagan priest. Moses's most controversial and darkest act was his later destruction of the Midianite nation.

8

The Burning Bush

LEADER:

Moses settled in Midian.
Life was comfortable,
life was sweet,
plenty to drink and eat.
Zipporah became his wife,
and he had kids,
Gershon and Eliezer.
What a life.
He tended his father-in-law's flocks;
no deadlines,
no clocks.
One day he saw a burning bush.
It would not extinguish,
very odd, very grim,
but then,
God spoke to him.

GOD:

Moses, my people are moaning.
In Egypt they are slaves.
They are suffering,
they're digging graves.
Be a gem:
rescue them.
Bring them to the land of milk and honey,
a land that's always sunny.

MOSES:

Hold on!
Why me?
I stutter,
I shudder.
I don't know about suffering,
grew up with a silver spoon
in a palace cocoon.
I don't have a feel for this.
I'm not amiss.
How will I convince anyone?
I'm a simple shepherd.
Pick someone with a better résumé,
me? No way!

GOD:

Moses, you forget who I am:
I'm God.
I created the world.
I perform miracles.
I am what I am.
This ain't a scam.
Pharaoh will bend;
this I contend.
You and me,
we'll set our people free.
You'll see.

MOSES:

I'm not a good talker,
I'm not a stalker.
I don't know what to say.
Where's the nearest subway?

GOD:

Take your brother Aaron.
He's a smoothie,
very groovy.
He'll talk for you.
Cheer up,
don't be blue.
Get your butt to Egypt—
you've got a job to do.

Source and Commentary: This narrative, referred to as 'The Call," is covered in Exodus 3 & Exodus 4. God said that he heard his people moaning and remembered his covenant with Abraham, Isaac, and Jacob (Exodus 2: 23-25). Does this imply that God forgot about his enslaved people and just now remembered their suffering? And why did it take 400 years for God to act? Another question is why did God choose Moses to lead this dangerous mission? What were Moses's qualifications? He was raised in splendor in an Egyptian palace, he probably committed murder, he was shy and unassuming, he wasn't a good talker or persuader, he was happy being a shepherd, nothing more, and, more importantly, he really didn't want the job. God saw something in Moses that he doesn't reveal. God would have made a great corporate head-hunter.

9

God Killing Moses

LEADER:

With his wife Zipporah and two boys, Moses left
the safety and comfort of his home in Midian and
headed hundreds of miles west to Egypt to free his
people. But he received a major shock at his first
encampment.

MOSES:

Wasn't my idea to go.
Happy to stay home,
you know.
So I'm on my way,
heading for Egypt,
not going to stray.
Now, here's the rub,
bub:
First night out,
I'm a real good scout.
God decides to kill me.
It's true!
Out of the blue.
What's going on?
Is this a con?
Am I gone?
But wait, you'll see.
A great idea—

how did she know?
My wife Zipporah
circumcises our boy.
So that's what it's all about?
No doubt!
That wife of mine,
A real gold mine.

Source and Commentary: If you don't believe it
could have happened, check out Exodus 4: 24-26.
This brutal, unexpected act by God has baffled
Biblical scholars for hundreds of years. God uses
his ultimate powers of persuasion to convince a
reluctant shepherd to leave the safety of his home
and schlep hundreds of miles away to free a million
people he doesn't really know or care about. Moses,
putting his faith in God, undertakes this very
problematic and dangerous mission. Then, when
Moses reaches the first encampment, God decides
to kill him simply because he failed to circumcise
his son. An interesting question one might ask is,
"Why didn't God bring this up before Moses left on
his journey?" It would have avoided a lot of
needless stress.

Moses Meets Pharaoh

LEADER: After a long journey from Midian,
Moses and his brother Aaron make it to Egypt. That
was the easy part. Convincing Pharaoh to free the
slaves—now that's going to require a few miracles
that only God can deliver. The negotiation begins.

MOSES to PHARAOH:

God has commanded,
demanded:
Let my people go.

PHARAOH:

Beg your pardon?
They are slaves,
knaves.
They provide free labor,
which is cool.
Free them?
I'm no fool.

MOSES:

They are suffering,
torture and woe.
So, in a nutshell,
let my people go.

PHARAOH:

Tell your God,
with displacements,
I'll need replacements.

MOSES:

No dice,
not nice.
Look, I turned a rod into a snake!
God is mighty;
he's no fake.

PHARAOH:

I don't give a lick.
My magicians can do the same trick.

MOSES:

Just going three days away,
Down the beltway,
Only to pray,
So, Pharaoh,
Watta you say?

PHARAOH:

You are interfering in our internal affairs,
violating international law,
which is the last straw.
You and your brother,
go back home.
It's overdue—
and take your stupid tricks with you.

Source and Commentary: The negotiation between
Moses and Pharaoh begins in Exodus 7: 1-13.
What's hard to fathom is how a disheveled, dust-
covered Moses, wearing tattered clothes, wangled
an audience with Pharaoh, perhaps the most
powerful monarch of that period. When Moses got
to the gate he was probably asked to state his
business. He might have replied, "My God and I
want Pharaoh to free his million-plus Hebrew
slaves." It's incredibly surprising that Pharaoh
agrees to see Moses. To free his people, Moses
realizes he'll need to be more Charleton Heston, and
he'll need major assistance from God. As every
Sunday-school kid knows, both happened.

11

The Ten Plagues

LEADER: Moses and God agreed. More than mere tired old tricks would be needed to sway Pharaoh to free the Israelite slaves. The canny Pharaoh also didn't buy Moses's promise that they would only travel three days away, pray, and then come back. God simply had to show Pharaoh who was the top honcho.

PHARAOH:

So you're back.

MOSES:

My God commands,
demands:
Let my people go.

PHARAOH:

You sound like a broken record.
Losing free labor, you know,
would cost me a lot of dough.
So the answer is still "No."

MOSES:

You underestimate our God.
He's gonna be mad—
watch what he'll do
to your people.
It'll be very sad.

ISRAELITE #1:

Plague #1.
God created the flood
a long time ago.
Now your water,
will turn to blood.

PHARAOH:

Okay, here's my plea:
Clear the water,
and your people will be free.

LEADER: The waters were cleared. No more
blood.

PHARAOH:

Blood in the water?
My magicians know this game.
They can do the same.
Sorry, I cannot agree.
Your people will not be free.

ISRAELITE #2:

Plague #2.
Frogs, frogs,
here, there, everywhere.

PHARAOH:

Okay. Here's my plea:
clear the frogs,
and your people will be free.

LEADER: The frogs were cleared.

PHARAOH:

My magicians know this game.
They can do the same.
Sorry, I cannot agree.
Your people will not be free.

ISRAELITE #3:

Plague #3.
Lice, lice,
like no other.
Everyone, take cover.

PHARAOH:

Okay. Here's my plea:
Clear the lice,
and your people will be free.

LEADER: The lice were cleared.

PHARAOH:

Can't stand lice,
but I'll sacrifice.
This I know,
your people will not go.

ISRAELITE #4:

Plague #4.
Insects, insects—
very sad.
They bite, they sting, they're very bad.

PHAROAH:

Enough already—
you win.
Clear the insects,
the exodus can begin.

LEADER: The insects were cleared.

PHARAOH:

Just kidding.
The insects were nothing.
Not even something.
Moses, call it a day;
just go away.

ISRAELITE #5:

Plague #5.
Pestilence.
Kill the livestock, cattle, and sheep.
Misery—
can't sleep.

PHARAOH:

Hah!
You think that's something?
You showed me nothing.
All my animals did not die,
Nice try.

ISRAELITE #1:

Plague #6.
Boils,
on the feet, hands, all over.
Moreover,
on the animals too.
That's what I'll do.

PHARAOH:

As you can see,
the boils are killing me.
So,
I'll let your people go.

LEADER: The boils were removed.

PHARAOH:

You cad,
The boils were not so bad.
No,
Your people can't go.

ISRAELITE #2:

Plague #7.
Hail, hail coming down
will destroy your wheat.
You'll have nothing to eat.

PHARAOH:

Tell your God,
let it be.
I'll take a plea.
Stop the hail,
and your people will be free.

LEADER: The hail stopped.

PHARAOH:

Your God,
stiffened my heart,
changed my mind.
I won't play this game.
The decision is the same:
It's crystal clear,
they stay right here.

ISRAELITE #3:

Plague #8.
Locusts from the sky.
Everyone's gonna die.
They'll eat everything in sight—
God is showing his might.

PHARAOH:

This is too much.
You're pounding away;
it's just not my day,
stop the locusts,
and your people are on their way.

LEADER: The locusts disappeared.

PHARAOH:

Your God is big and strong,
but he's wrong.
He's playing games with me.
No *way* your people will be free.

ISRAELITE #4:

Plague #9.
Darkness, no light.
Pharaoh, do what's right.
Don't fiddle with God's might.

PHARAOH:

Don't harden my heart.
I know when I'm beat.
Make light again,
Amen.

LEADER: The darkness became light.

PHARAOH:

He's done it again,
hardened my heart.
This you should fear:
you're all gonna die here.

ISRAELITE #5:

Plague #10.
The final one.
Your first born will die.
Many will cry,
don't be a schmo,
let my people go.

PHARAOH:

Have them pack up and leave.
I will not grieve.
They want liberation?
Maybe form a nation?
I offer them emancipation.

ISRAELITES (as a group):

And we departed.
Freedom—
Can we handle it?
Can we bear it?
Four hundred years being slaves;
Can we cope?
Can't mope,
let's just hope.

Source and Commentary: The redactors gave much space in the Torah to the ten plagues. This tale is also the highlight of the Passover Haggadah. It's covered in Exodus 7: 15-29, and Exodus 8, 9, 10, and 11. Many question the fact that in the last four plagues it appears that Pharaoh is ready to concede defeat and let the Israelites depart. However, each of these times, God stiffens (and hardens) Pharaoh's heart, which forces him to change his mind. In doing so, it seems that God may not believe that we all have "free will." Even though there are many explanations for what happens in this story, God makes it crystal clear why he hardened Pharaoh's heart and why he wanted ten plagues: "I have done so to show them my power and that my fame may resound throughout the world. And that I may display my signs." (Exodus 10: 1-3). A psychotherapist might suggest that, in these instances, God lacks a bit of self-esteem. On another question, some ethicists claim that Moses lied when he told Pharaoh that his sole intention was to take his people just three days away so they can pray to God. But, to quote the last line from the film *Some Like It Hot*, "Nobody's perfect!"

12

Departing Egypt

LEADER:

600,000 men left Egypt,
not counting women and children.
They had been slaves for 430 years.
Very cruel, very wrong.
What took God so long?
Before leaving, they borrowed gold and silver
from their friendly neighbors.
Were they greedy?
Or just needy.

PHARAOH (to his troops):

I'm changing my mind,
Free labor is hard to find!
Arm the chariots,
pursue them,
bring them back.
Every Jill and Jack.
Don't stall—
kill them all.

LEADER:

But God was not through.
He'd show Pharaoh a thing or two.
He had a plan:
destroy Pharaoh's army,
every last man.

GOD to MOSES:

Moses, here's what to do:
halt your march,
head back,
make sure Pharaoh sees you.
The Red Sea is at your back.
I'll part it,
you cross it.
Don't delay.
Trust me:
Pharaoh is history.
When he tries to cross the river,
it will not part.
His men will drown.
That's the lowdown.
The world will see my might:
it will shine like a bright light.

Source and Commentary: Exodus 14: 1-31. The
story of the departure from Egypt and the parting of
the Red Sea is well known. I do, however, have
essential questions about this segment: (1) Was it
necessary for the author to write that upon

departing, the Israelites "borrowed" objects of silver and gold from their Egyptian neighbors? (Exodus 12:35). Did the Israelites intend to return the stuff? Or was this part of God's promise to Abraham that his people will depart Egypt with "great wealth" (Exodus 15: 13). This passage has given ammunition to anti-Semites. (2) Didn't God set up the Red Sea confrontation by instructing Moses to turn back? The reason, of course, was to entice the Egyptians to pursue the Israelites. And, by doing so, the Egyptians all drowned in the Red Sea. The Biblical scholars offer unsatisfactory answers to these two questions. Today we would say, "they do a lot of spinning."

13

In the Wilderness

LEADER:

The forty years in the desert were nightmare years
for the Israelites. They were often demoralized.
They withstood periods of hunger and thirst. Moses
and God were exasperated and often lacked
compassion.

ISRAELITES to MOSES:

Take us back!
Yes, we'll be slaves,
but here in the desert
we're digging our graves.
Back in Egypt,
there's plenty to eat.
In the desert,
we face defeat.
Great, we're God's creation;
meanwhile, we're facing starvation.

LEADER:

In the wilderness,
God pointed the way.
A pillar of cloud
by day.
A flash of fire
by night.

ISRAELITES:

Moses, here's the bit,
face it:
we're running out of water,
out of food.
Don't mean to be rude,
take care of your brood.
Four hundred years of slavery—
now this?
This freedom ain't bliss.

MOSES:

You're all cowards.
No will!
Stop squawking,
I've had my fill.
This slave mentality,
let it go.
You're all complainers,
from head to toe.

LEADER:

The complaints didn't stop.
No water, no food,
and nowhere to shop.
But God was nearby,
water poured from the rocks.
Manna bread and quail fell from the sky.
Moses and God,
came through.
They are our glue.

Source and Commentary: Exodus 15: 22-27 &
Exodus 16: 1-16. Throughout the forty years of
wandering, the demoralized Israelites are a handful,
constantly complaining and asking to go back to the
safety of Egypt. It occurs to me that both Moses and
God do not understand the huge adjustment the
Israelites face. Having known only slavery, they are
suddenly rescued by a phantom leader who keeps
telling them to believe in a God they can't see or
understand. What the Israelites need most from
Moses and God is a bit of slack. A bit of
understanding. At this point God does not inform
his people that the journey to The Promised Land
will take 40 years. After all, caravans, nomadic
tribes, and even Moses (when he escaped from
Egypt) crossed the Sinai in a few weeks. Would the
Israelites have consented to the "rescue" if they
knew they would be wandering (and dying) in the
desert wilderness for so many years?

14

Rock Turns to Water

LEADER:

The wandering was torture.
No water, no chow.

ISRAELITES:

So, what now?

MOSES to GOD:

They're complaining all the time.
God, we need an answer,
preferably before nighttime.

ISRAELITE #1:

We never should have come.

ISRAELITE #2:

Real dumb.

ISRAELITE #3:

We're starving.

ISRAELITE #4:

We're crying.

ISRAELITE #5:

Worse. We're dying.

GOD to MOSES:

They lost faith in me,
don't deserve to be free.
I have to show them a thing or two—
here's what I'm going to do:

Moses, see that rock over there?
Smack it.
Presto.
Water, water everywhere.
I'm God almighty;
never take me lightly.

Source and Commentary: Exodus 17: 3-7. We
witness a trick God will perform one more time,
namely getting water by smacking a rock. More
importantly, God sometimes wants you to do this
trick a certain way. Woe to the person who fails to
follow God's precise instructions. Later in the
journey, at Meribah-kadesh, the Israelites again are
dying from thirst. Moses produces water, but he will
pay a very dear price for a seemingly trivial
transgression.

15

War with the Amalekites

LEADER: After months hardening up in the Sinai, God felt the Israelites were ready to do battle with one of the troublemaking tribes that roamed the desert, the Amalekites. He knew the Israelites would have to fight their way past many ruthless enemies before reaching The Promised Land. This battle would test their mettle. Were they ready to fight, or would they run for the hills? As the saying goes, "With God's help, great things can happen."

GOD to MOSES:

The Amalekites are looking to fight.
It's going to be quite a sight.
Arm your troops, get them ready—
be quick, but steady.
Moses, listen to me:
Go to the top of the hill.
Raise your hands,
Israelites win the war;
lower your hands,
defeat will occur.

MOSES to JOSHUA:

Joshua,
got the word from above.
No time to drill,
attack at will.

MOSES (to the troops):

I'm old.
Got to keep my hands up—
can't let up,
Someone, help keep my hands up
so we can clean up.

LEADER:

And so it went.
The Israelites won their first war.
Have a cigar.
Joshua's now a star.
What a victory,
total glee.
Here's why:
God was their ally.

Source and Commentary: Exodus 17: 8-16. The
Torah does state that the Israelites and Amalekites
had tussled before at Rephidim. So this could be
considered the battle to forever silence a
troublesome enemy. Contrary to Biblical lore, the
Sinai desert was not a totally barren wilderness.

Caravans often traversed it, and roaming nomadic tribes were an ongoing threat. However, the Amalekites were considered the Israelites' arch enemy, and they would be so for the entire journey. From this battle, a great Israelite hero emerges: Joshua. At the end of their journey, Joshua, not Moses, will be the one God taps to lead the Israelites into The Promised Land.

16

Jethro Visits Moses

LEADER: Jethro, Moses's wife Zipporah, and their
two boys, Gershon and Eliezer, visit him in his
encampment in the Sinai desert. Noteworthy is
Jethro's MBA lesson to Moses on the subject of
business management.

JETHRO to MOSES:

Proud of your success, m'boy:
victory over Egypt,
victory over the Amalekites.
What stress,
but what a success.

I'm on my way to see you.
With me, know who?
Zipporah and your sons.

MOSES:

Welcome to my tent.
I'm up to my neck;
working here is making me a wreck.
Decisions every day.
What can I say?

JETHRO:

You're doing it all wrong,
killing yourself.
Don't be a jerk—
delegate the work.
Pick division leaders,
take them aside,
hand them smaller disputes.
These they can decide.
This will take a load off your back.
Now you won't crack.

LEADER:

Moses took the advice,
and bid Jethro and his family
a safe journey back.

Source and Commentary: Exodus 18: 1-27. Moses
rarely displayed deep affection for anyone near him.
He doesn't express love, or even any interest, in his
parents, his wife Zipporah, his two boys, or his
brother Aaron and sister Miriam. And, of course,
his relationship with God is volatile, to say the least.
The sole person, it seems, that Moses cares much
about is his father-in-law Jethro. It's a relationship
not often discussed by the Biblical scholars. But it
does seem like a very special one. Jethro is
concerned when he sees Moses heading for an
emotional breakdown in a time before Prozac. And,
like a good mentor, he gives Moses an insightful

lesson in how he should manage his business. Also, take note of how easily Jethro travels with his daughter and two grandsons, crossed the Sinai to visit Moses. No sweat. And yet, here is Moses wandering around for forty years over the same desert. Perhaps one can say that Moses simply had a bad sense of direction. A baffling side of Moses (and a bloodthirsty one) is later depicted when he orders the destruction of Jethro's people, the Midianites, for a relatively minor transgression.

17

The Covenant

GOD to MOSES:

Come to my office on Mount Sinai.
We have to talk—
run, don't walk!

MOSES to ISRAELITES:

Heading to meet God.
Aaron's in charge.
Be brave,
and most of all,
behave!

GOD to MOSES:

Business first.
Here's my covenant.
Let everyone know:
Obey me faithfully.
Be good,
as you should,
and you'll be my treasured people.
Understood?

LEADER: Moses came down from the mountain
and, as God requested, informed his people.

ISRAELITES:

All that God has spoken,
we'll do.
Moses,
we're with you.

Source and Commentary: Exodus 19: 1-25. The
covenant is the start of a relationship that will go
through many peaks and valleys. The Israelites
often forget their end of the deal, and God (contrary
to Biblical assurances) will not always be "slow to
anger and quick to forget."

18

The Golden Calf

LEADER:

Again,
Moses goes to the top of Mount Sinai,
where he can almost touch the sky.
Clouds and thunder all over,
but Moses doesn't stir,
cools his heels for six days.
He's in a daze.
On the 7th day,
God appears.
Cheers.
Thought the meeting would last a day?
It lasted forty days.
What can I say?

ISRAELITES to AARON:

Moses ain't coming down soon.
It's over, our honeymoon.
Aaron, don't be a clod—
find us another god.

AARON to ISRAELITES:

Your gold and jewelry,
hand them over.
I'll melt them down
and mold a golden calf.
Don't laugh.
What a great day!
This is your new god;
Go now and pray.

ISRAELITES:

Tomorrow we'll feast and drink.
We now have a god that we can see.
We don't need to see a shrink.
Great to be free.

GOD to MOSES:

Moses,
look what's happening below.
You should only know:
my people are worshipping another god,
a demigod.
What gall!
I'll kill them all.

MOSES to GOD:

Hold on—not so fast.
Be steadfast.
Pharaoh will say you freed them,
and now you kill them?
Not good publicity.
Hold on; that's my plea.

GOD to MOSES:

You punish them.
Get it done,
my dear son.

MOSES to GOD:

I'll smash the tablets;
that's just the beginning.
Many must die for their sinning.
Three thousand, at least,
men, women, children, and beast.

MOSES to AARON:

Aaron, you let me down,
you clown.
Why did you do it?
You twit.

AARON to MOSES:

You know they were so sad,
unruly and bad.
So I did it.
I threw the gold into the fire,
and a golden calf popped out.
Just like that,
like a rabbit out of a hat.

MOSES to AARON:

You expect me to believe that spin?
You can't win.
You're my brother,
so you're not going to die.
But remember this:
it's not who you are,
but who you know,
so, go!

GOD to MOSES:

These people,
we should forgive and forget.
The guilty have died,
so take it in stride.
Let's move on.
Doggone!

Source and Commentary: Exodus 32: 1-33. Worshipping the Golden Calf represents the biggest betrayal to date of God's covenant with the Israelites. Two questions should be asked: (1) Moses deserves credit for dissuading a furious God from destroying the entire nation. However, Moses did execute 3,000 of his people. Among those executed were "brother, neighbor, and kin." Therefore, tragically, many who were innocent died "by association." Did Moses go too far? (2) Aaron was the ringleader. Why did Moses spare his life? Why wasn't he, at least, punished? Instead, he was elevated to high priest. Like today, it's good to know someone in high places.

19

The Ten Commandments

LEADER: Three times, Moses trekked back and forth between the top of Mount Sinai and his people below, conveying God's instructions. The third time up, God was ready for some serious business. He dictated to Moses the 613 laws, the first ten being The Ten Commandments. God was adamant and rigid that his Commandments be followed. "My way or the highway." Disobeying these Commandments often meant death. However, if followed, God would embrace the Israelites as his treasured possession, His Chosen People.

To be contrary,
each Commandment,
includes a commentary.
Of what people would say,
in the world today.

GOD to MOSES:

I'm ready to go.
My first ten commandments,
603 more to follow.

MOSES to GOD:

Ready for dictation—
what a great occasion.

GOD:

#1. You shall have no other God beside me.

ISRAELITE #1:

But if I prefer worshiping another god,
Don't spank me with your rod.

GOD:

#2. You shall not make a sculptured image.

ISRAELITE #2:

Maybe it'll be a piece of art—
have a heart!

GOD:

#3. You shall not swear in my name.

ISRAELITE #3:

A friendly swear does no harm.
It's part of my charm.

GOD:

#4. Observe the Sabbath and keep it holy.

ISRAELITE #4:

If I do not work that day,
there'll be bills I cannot pay.

GOD:

#5. Honor your father and mother.

ISRAELITE #5:

Not if they are rarely seen;
not if they're cruel and mean.

GOD:

#6. You shall not murder.

ISRAELITE #1:

It's not right, one bit.
Even if Moses did it.

GOD:

#7. You shall not steal.

ISRAELITE #2:

Charging more than you should?
That's stealing. Not good.

GOD:

#8. Do not covet your neighbor's house, possessions, or wife.

ISRAELITE #3:

It can destroy a nation.
Cool off, take a vacation.

GOD:

#9. Do not commit adultery.

ISRAELITE #4:

This kind of love?
See Commandment #8 above.

GOD:

#10. Do not bear false witness against your neighbor.

ISRAELITE #5:

It's not a small detail.
Innocent people end up in jail.

Source and Commentary: Exodus 20: 1-7 and
Exodus 20: 12-18. Without a doubt, The Ten

Commandments represent the solid foundation of the Jewish, Christian and Islamic civilizations. It should be understood that The Ten Commandments were set forth (either by God or a redactor) thousands of years ago when a different set of morality and ethics applied. Today, no person fears death if any Commandment is disobeyed. We do, however, consider them a valuable set of rules that make our civilization bearable.

20

Military Intelligence

LEADER: The invasion of Canaan was imminent.
God wanted Moses to gather intelligence on the
strength of the enemy and the condition of the land
for farming and grazing.

GOD to MOSES:

Before invading Canaan,
we need military intelligence.
Know your enemy.
Will they fight or flee?
Are they strong and big?
Or will they break like a twig?
Find all this out;
have no doubt.

LEADER:

Moses did just that—sent out scouts. After forty
days of observing, they returned with this report.

SCOUTS to MOSES:

We're back.
Here's our feedback:
Truly, a land of milk and honey,
but our enemies are fierce and tough,
very rough.
Better we stay right here,
in the rear,
safe and clear.

CALEB (a scout) to MOSES:

Hell no!
Let's go!
We can beat them,
destroy them.
God's on our side—
Let's not hide.

ISRAELITES to MOSES:

Take us back to Egypt,
we'll again be slaves;
here in the desert,
we're digging our graves.

GOD to MOSES:

My people don't trust me.
Let them be.
They'll never see The Promised Land;
they'll all die in the Sinai sand.
As for the scouts who feared the enemy?
Blasphemy.
My plague will kill everyone.
I'm done.

Source and Commentary: Reconnaissance of Canaan is covered in Numbers 13: 1-33 and Numbers 14: 1-37. Knowing that destruction of the enemy is certain, it's puzzling that God asks Moses to check them out. Perhaps He is testing the fortitude of the Israelites after hearing the scary report from the scouts. The decision by God to kill the scouts, who gave the negative report, with the usual plague (Numbers 14:37) seems harsh. We also learn, once more, that God is determined that none of the slaves who left Egypt with Moses will live to see The Promised Land. The sole exceptions are Joshua and Caleb. In fact, right from the beginning, He decided that His people, possessing a slave-mentality, would not be able to fight their way to The Promised Land. It's also the most persuasive explanation of why God decided to have His people roam the Sinai desert for 40 years.

21

Overthrowing Moses—Aaron and Miriam

LEADER: It's been said over and over again: family members shouldn't work in the same office. Often they get on each other's nerves. Or worse.

MOSES:

No! No! No!
My brother Aaron, my sister Miriam,
they want me to go,
to overthrow me.
God is the key
to help me.

AARON and MIRIAM:

Yes, Moses has to go,
married a Cushite woman,
yes, that's so.
Thinks he's so great—
that's what we hate.
Speaks to God alone.
Hey, bro,
you're not on any throne.
Forgot about us?
No fuss,
just let us know.
When are you going to go?

GOD to AARON and MIRIAM:

Aaron, I want to know:
you want your brother to go?
How dare you!
You weren't raised in a zoo.
And, Miriam—
shame on you.
Leprosy, I'll give you.
Aaron, as for you,
I expected more.
You were my core.
Feel guilty for being remiss;
now you'll have to live with this.

MOSES to GOD:

Miriam has leprosy.
Give her a break,
for my sake.
She tried to overthrow me,
Let her be.
Make her well,
she is kinda swell.

GOD to MIRIAM:

Miriam,
get away for seven days.
Be assured,
you will be cured.

LEADER:

Aaron got a pass,
no doubt.
Let the Rabbis figure that one out.

Source and Commentary: Numbers 12: 1-16. If ever
there was a teflon man in the Torah, Aaron wins,
hands down. He beats the rap with the Golden Calf.
And he beats the rap with the above insurrection.
And he becomes God's High Priest. Incredibly,
today, many revere him. I have not heard or read a
cogent explanation of how this guy pulled it off.

22

Overthrowing Moses—Korah

LEADER:

Here we go again,
another coup.
Like the cavalry,
God to the rescue.

KORAH to MOSES:

You want to be
so high and mighty,
to talk to God alone.
To Him, we're unknown.
Many support us—
that's a plus.
Moses, it's over.
No slur,
we're takin' over.

MOSES:

Hah! What a joke,
you bloke.
God's on my side,
so go take a ride.
Don't persist—
desist.
If you don't fly,
you'll all die.

KORAH:

I don't care,
I don't scare,
don't give a damn.
We're not going to scram.

GOD to MOSES:

I hear what's goin' on.
Whereupon,
I'll make them crawl,
then crush them all.
Now, Moses, listen to me:
Get your people away
from Korah and his gang.
The ground below them
will crack,
swallow them up.
No need to flee.
Is God great?
Mais oui!

Source and Commentary: Numbers 16: 1-35. God
spared the lives of Aaron and Miriam for their
insurrection. Not so with Korah and his co-
conspirators. Not a good example of equal justice
under the law. Then, unmercifully, He had the
ground open up and swallow Korah and his gang,
including their "wives, sons, and little ones."
Another example of punishment by association.

23

The Sin of Moses

LEADER: Herein lies the tragedy of Moses: The man did everything God requested and then some…

ISRAELITES (one by one):

He enforced all of God's laws and instructions.

He was loyal to the ultimate degree.

He was a beloved friend.

He spoke to God face to face.

He left his tranquil life as a shepherd to endure forty nightmare years in the desert.

LEADER:

…but all this was forgotten because of one trivial act of disobedience.

ISRAELITES to MOSES:

Meribah-kadesh, oh shucks,
this place sucks!
No water, no denyin'
we're dyin'.

We're outta here,
packin' our gear,
no regrets, no fear.

GOD to MOSES:

My people have stiff necks—
what wrecks.
Moses, listen to me:
that rock over there,
talk to it.
Water will pour out,
and bring an end to the drought.

MOSES to ISRAELITES:

Hear ye. Watch this.
I'll strike the rock with my rod,
as instructed by God.
Done.
Water, water now,
for everyone.

GOD to MOSES:

Moses, you creep,
were you asleep?
I said *talk* to the rock,
not *strike* the rock.
So I have to make this stand:
You ain't goin' to The Promised Land.

MOSES:

God expects nothing less,
I forgot.
A sad, tragic mess.

Source and Commentary: Numbers 20: 6-13 and
Deuteronomy 32: 51-52. There has been an
enormous amount of discussion about why God did
not want Moses to enter The Promised Land.
There were a great many theories and explanations.
But God's justification is crystal clear: "For you
broke faith with Me at the waters of Meribath-
kadesh. You may view the land from a distance, but
you shall not enter it---the land I am giving to the
Israelite people." (Deuteronomy 32: 51-53). That's
it. The only reason. End of discussion.

24

The Midian Massacre

LEADER:

In the land of Moab, shortly before the big invasion,
Midianite women seduced Israelite soldiers and
showed them their pagan idols. God was furious.
Plague time. Twenty-four thousand Midianites died.
But God was still not satisfied—the worst was yet
to come. He instructed Moses to finish them off.
Would Moses forget he was sheltered by a
Midianite family after escaping Egypt? That his
wife Zipporah was a Midianite?

GOD to MOSES:

Don't tell your wife,
Zipporah, the Midianite,
that I'm killing her entire tribe.
That's my last word—
get your sword.

MOSES to ISRAELITE SOLDIERS:

God has spoken
With quite a shrill.
The Midianites,
kill, kill, kill!

LEADER: Days later.

We did it,
every bit.
Killed every man,
from every clan.

MOSES to ISRAELITE SOLDIERS:

Damn!
That's no coup.
Women and children,
kill them too.
Virgin women only—
they can live.

LEADER:

The Midianites were massacred
by order of Moses.
Wonder how Zipporah felt?
Divorce?
Cost him a lot of gelt.

Source and Commentary: Numbers 31: 1-18. This
event somewhat defames the otherwise worthy life
of Moses. Why would he be so brutal and cruel to a
people who sheltered him after his escape from
Egypt? His wife and his beloved father-in-law,
Jethro, were Midianites. Moses, who never
hesitated to cool down God when He was in one of
his most vindictive moods, failed to do so in this

instance. Worse, he didn't even try. The men came back and reported that they had killed all of the Midianite men and destroyed all the towns. Mission accomplished. Moses was not satisfied. He berated them and ordered them to go back and kill the women and children. The only ones he spared were virgin women. Question? Weren't the Israelites who were seduced by the captivating Midianite women just as guilty?

25

The Invasion

LEADER:

And, finally, what began with the liberation of the
Israelites at the Sea of Reeds forty years ago
reached its final stage on the banks of the Jordan
River. Invasion and conquest was now at hand, as
God had promised. And yet, God deliberately made
sure that not one of the Israelite slaves who left
Egypt got to see The Promised Land, except Caleb
and Joshua. All of them, more than a million men,
women, and children, perished in the desert.

MOSES:

I wonder,
knowing this,
would they have followed me?
In the wilderness forty years,
crying bitter tears,
digging their graves—
would they have been better
remaining as slaves?

GOD to MOSES:

Your people are ready:
Young, tough, and strong.
Very steady—
it won't be long,
Joshua to command,
make your stand.
Conquest and elimination,
extermination.
That's what they gotta do.
I promise you this:
Destroy them, or I'll destroy you.

Dear Moses, one last word:
Take off your sword,
climb Mount Nebo.
I want you to see
the vast Promised Land.
Now, Moses,
understand:
you ain't goin' to enter this land.
That's all.
On Mount Nebo, you will die,
on Mount Nebo, you will fall.

Source and Commentary: Numbers 27: 12-23.
There's something sadistic about God insisting that
Moses see The Promised Land, and then telling
him, "Know this, that land, you shall not go over."
(Deuteronomy 34:4). God forgave many of his
people who disobeyed Him or even violated His

laws. And yet, God's unmerciful punishment of Moses, for committing a trivial transgression, is beyond comprehension. What happened to the saying that "God was quick to forget?" We also see the ruthless side of God when he commands that the Israelites destroy everyone occupying the land. As written in Deuteronomy 20:16, "You shall not let a soul remain alive."

26

The Death of Moses

GOD to MOSES:

Moses,
the day has come when you must die.

LEADER:

Like a corporate CEO,
God made his decision,
got rid of Moses.
Pretty cold,
but Moses disobeyed God's order,
and, furthermore,
he was too old.
Replaced with a young buck,
Joshua.

ISRAELITES:

Good choice.
A war hero—
what luck.

MOSES to JOSHUA:

Joshua, take my sword.
But one last word:
have courage and stay strong.
God wasn't wrong.
You'll be all right.
I pray for you
with all my might.

MOSES to GOD:

Dear God,
before I die,
let me enter The Promised Land.
I'm gonna cry.
Let me go—
I want to know.

GOD to MOSES:

Speak no more.
You know the score.
Listen to what I said,
get it in your head,
you're not entering The Promised Land.
That's my final stand.

LEADER: With Moses's death imminent, we
realize what a complicated man he was, volatile at
times, but always humble.

ISRAELITES #1:

He was as unassuming and humble as Mahatma Ghandi.

ISRAELITES #2:

As ruthless as Attila the Hun.

ISRAELITES #3:

As great a tactician as Otto von Bismarck.

ISRAELITES #4:

As demanding as a Marine drill sergeant.

ISRAELITES #5:

A leader of the oppressed, comparable to Martin Luther King.

LEADER:

Civilization as we know it today
began with God's laws,
enforced by Moses,
promulgated thousands of years ago.
And they are still right on the dough.

ISRAELITE #1:

"Do not bear false witness"…

ISRAELITE #2:

…should be in the head of every person testifying in court.

ISRAELITE #3:

"Justice, justice shalt thou follow"…

ISRAELITE #4:

…continues to be the battle cry of the Civil Rights Movement.

ISRAELITE #5:

"Honor thy father and mother"…

ISRAELITE #1:

…could prevent a lot of the juvenile crime we see today.

ISRAELITE #2:

"Love ye the stranger, for you were strangers in the land of Egypt"…

ISRAELITE #3:

…could shape more compassionate legislation on immigration.

ISRAELITE #4:

"Do not steal" and "Do not murder"…

ISRAELITE #5:

…are basic laws in every civilized country.

ISRAELITE #1:

"Just balance, just weights you shall have in your markets."

ISRAELITE #2:

Merchants, storekeepers: remember this law!

ISRAELITE #3:

"Set a percentage of your harvest for the poor"…

ISRAELITE #4:

…Yes! It's the "haves" helping the "have nots".

LEADER: Moses's obituary can be read in Deuteronomy 34: 1-10. And so, Moses died in Moab, alone. As God ordained, he never entered The Promised Land. Such is the tragedy of Moses. To this day, archeologists have not discovered his grave or any evidence of his existence. Perhaps, that's the way God wanted it to be.

Moses was 120 years old.

Notes

Notes

Notes

Notes

Made in the USA
Middletown, DE
10 February 2017